HOW TO LEAD WHEN YOU'RE NOT IN CHARGE

LEVERAGING INFLUENCE
WHEN YOU LACK AUTHORITY

BIBLE STUDY GUIDE | 6 SESSIONS
UPDATED EDITION

CLAY SCROGGINS

HarperChristian Resources

How to Lead When You're Not in Charge Bible Study Guide, Updated Edition

Copyright © 2018 by Clay Scroggins

Published by HarperChristian Resources, 3950 Sparks Drive SE, Suite 101, Grand Rapids, MI 49546, USA. HarperChristian Resources is a registered trademark of HarperCollins Christian Publishing, Inc.

Requests for information should be sent to customercare@harpercollins.com.

ISBN 978-0-310-18389-1 (softcover)
ISBN 978-0-310-18390-7 (ebook)

HarperCollins Publishers, Macken House, 39/40 Mayor Street Upper, Dublin 1, D01 C9W8, Ireland (https://www.harpercollins.com).

Cover Design: Tammy Johnson
Interior Design: Kait Lamphere

First Printing March 2018

CONTENTS

ABOUT THE STUDY

I've always wanted to be a leader. I imagine you have as well. For me, it began in elementary school. I wanted so badly to be the captain of the Safety Patrol. There was something alluring about the bright sash I got to wear. There was something powerful about being able to stop tons of steel and plastic with a raised hand. I just knew if I was captain of the Safety Patrol, it would change the way people saw me, and it would even change the way I saw myself.

When I was in high school, I ran for class president. I had this idea to mix up famous hip-hop songs with my campaign slogans. I did a mash-up of "Back That Thang Up" and Vote for Clay for President. Unfortunately, it worked.

That intense desire to lead followed me into college and my first job. To a certain extent, that desire is natural. We all want it to some degree or another. And that's because we associate leadership with autonomy. If we're the leader, we get to call our own shots. We get to shape our own universe. We're answerable to no one. And only when we have that kind of total freedom can we reach our full potential as leaders. That's what we assume.

But here's the dirty little secret we're going to explore in this study: Autonomy is a myth. Every person who climbs the leadership ladder must eventually face the truth that everyone is accountable to someone. Even the CEO with the corner office, corporate jet, and multimillion-dollar salary is accountable to the board of directors and the shareholders of the company they lead.

Autonomy is a unicorn. It doesn't exist. If you spend your life or career chasing it in your spheres of influence, you'll never reach your full potential as a leader. You just won't.

But here's the good news: There's a better way. When you abandon the hunt for autonomy, it can shift the focus of your leadership fundamentally. It can open the door to your full leadership potential.

That will require changing some of the ways you think about leadership, as well as some of the things you currently do as a leader.

That's what we're going to explore during the six sessions of this study.

HOW TO USE THIS GUIDE

This study can be used by groups of all different sizes. But we think the ideal is a group of eight to twelve adults or four to six married couples. Why? Because that's a large enough group to provide the diverse opinions that drive dynamic conversation, but small enough that group members can hold one another accountable.

Accountability is absolutely crucial to the group dynamic. Reading this material, watching the videos, and having some discussions probably won't create a big, sustainable change to your leadership. That will only happen if you *apply* what you learn. And you will probably succeed in application only if you have a group of people who are willing to encourage you and hold you accountable.

So, while the videos are available for you to view at any time (see the instructions provided with this guide), we encourage you to go through this content with a *group*. This could be a Bible study, Sunday school class, or any other gathering that you want to put together. Here is a basic overview of what you can expect during your time together.

GROUP STUDY

Each of the sessions in this study is divided into two parts: (1) a group study section and (2) a personal study section. The group study section provides a basic framework on how to open your time together, get the most out of the video content, and discuss the key ideas that were presented in the teaching. The suggested meeting time each week is ninety minutes. This can be broken down as follows:

- **Welcome** and **Overview**: An opening note about the topic of the session and what will be covered for you to read on your own.
- **Connect** (*10 minutes*): This conversation starter is designed to tee up the session's topic while helping you get to know one another a little better. This is especially helpful if your group is new.
- **Watch** (*15 minutes*): This section includes a summary of what you will watch in the video teaching along with space for you to take notes.
- **Discuss** (*45 minutes*): You will want to spend most of the session having a conversation about the content you just watched. Use any or all of the questions provided to guide the conversation.
- **Challenge** (*15 minutes*): This leadership challenge, which you will do on your own, provides a simple way to begin applying what you're learning. Don't skip this section of the study. It will help you change and grow.
- **Close** (*5 minutes*): The closing wrap-up will help you put a bow on the session, so to speak. It's an opportunity to reiterate the bottom line of the session's topic. It's also an opportunity to close the meeting in prayer.

Make sure you have your own copy of the study guide so you can write down your thoughts, responses, and reflections—and so you have access to the videos via streaming. You may also want to have a copy of the *How to Lead When You're Not in Charge* book. This is optional for the group meetings but highly recommended for the between-sessions study. One copy per couple is fine. (See the notes at the beginning of each group session on which chapters of the book you should read before the next group session.)

Finally, keep these points in mind:

- **Facilitation**: You will want to appoint someone to serve as a facilitator. This person will be responsible for starting the video and keeping track of time during discussions and activities. If you have been chosen for this role, there are some resources in the back of this guide that can help you lead your group through the study.
- **Faithfulness**: Your group is a place where tremendous growth can happen as you reflect on the Bible, ask questions, and learn what God is doing in other people's lives. For this

reason, be fully committed and attend each session so you can build trust and rapport with the other members.

- **Friendship:** The goal of any small group is to serve as a place where people can share, learn about God, and build friendships. So make your group a safe place. Be honest about your thoughts and feelings, but also listen to everyone else's thoughts, feelings, and opinions. Keep anything personal your group members share in confidence so you can create a community where people can heal, be challenged, and grow spiritually.

PERSONAL STUDY

The personal study is for you to work through on your own during the week. Each exercise is designed to help you explore the key ideas you uncovered during your group time and delve into passages of Scripture that will help you apply those principles to your life. Go at your own pace, doing a little each day—or tackle the material all at once. Remember to spend a few moments in silence to listen to whatever God might be saying to you.

If you are unable to finish (or even start) these weekly personal studies, you should still attend the group time. Be assured you are still wanted and welcome even if you don't have your "homework" done. The personal studies are simply intended to help you to dive deeper into what God's Word has to say about leadership and how to apply those truths to your life. So, as you go through this study, be listening for how God will change some of the ways you think about leadership and challenge what you are currently doing as a leader.

WEEK 1
AT A GLANCE

This Week's Reading:	Chapters 1–3 in *How to Lead When You're Not in Charge*
Group Meeting:	Read the Welcome and Connect with the group (page 2)
	Watch the video and take notes (pages 3–4)
	Discuss the questions that follow (page 5)
	Respond to the teaching and Close (page 6)
Personal Study:	
Study 1	Read and answer the questions on chapter 1 (pages 8–9)
Study 2	Respond to a related passage from the Bible (pages 10–11)
Study 3	Reflect on what you've studied this week (page 12)
Catch Up and Read Ahead	Connect with someone in your group during the week
(before week 2 group meeting)	Complete any unfinished studies (page 13)
Next Week's Reading	Chapter 4 in *How to Lead When You're Not in Charge*

THE ODDITY OF LEADERSHIP

Many people at the top of organizations are not leaders. They have authority, but they are not leaders. And many at the bottom with no authority are absolutely leaders.

SIMON SINEK

WELCOME

Welcome to *How to Lead When You're Not in Charge*! My hope in this study is to set the table for some terrific group discussion and exercises that will help you put action to the ideas in my book of the same name. My life experiences have taught me that the greatest growth usually comes in the context of relationships with others. And my hope is the same for you as you work through this study guide!

If you haven't met as a group, make sure to go around the room and introduce yourselves. And maybe even make an agreement with one another that might go like this: *I'm going to be as honest as I can be over the next several weeks. And if you agree to that as well, I'll agree to let what's said in here stay in here. In doing so, we can create something akin to the Las Vegas of leadership studies!*

OVERVIEW

Great leaders do not wait to be in charge before they start leading. By cultivating and leveraging influence, great leaders learn to lead before ever landing in any position of authority. In order to begin to lead when you're not in charge, you must debunk the myth that authority is a prerequisite for influence. If having authority doesn't necessarily mean you have any influence, it must be possible to have influence before ever having authority. If this is true, it really changes everything about leadership.

CONNECT

Briefly discuss your first memory of wanting to lead.

WATCH

Watch the video for this session, which you can access through streaming (see the instructions provided with this guide). A summary is provided for your benefit as well as space to take additional notes.

SUMMARY

Maybe you've always wanted to be a leader or maybe you've only led reluctantly. Maybe somebody—a parent, teacher, or coach—pointed out your leadership potential early in life or maybe you still don't think of yourself as a leader. Regardless of your specific circumstances, you *are* a leader in some sphere of your life—in your career, at church, or in your home.

Given the fact that you are responsible for leading someone, don't you want to lead as well as you can?

One of the most important things you can do to amp up your leadership ability is to understand the difference between *authority* and *leadership*.

Because of what we experience as kids, we associate authority and leadership. Growing up, whether your parents were good leaders or not, they had authority over you. They had all of the money. They put a roof over your head. They put food on the table. They had control.

So, it's natural for us to confuse authority and leadership. But one of the oddest truths I've bumped into in my career is that the more authority I've been given, the more clearly I've been able to see the difference between authority and leadership.

We may be tempted to believe that the people with the corner offices, best parking spots, and highest positions on the organization chart must be great leaders. We may be tempted to believe that authority is leadership. But being given authority doesn't automatically make you a great leader.

Imagine a steering wheel. Now think about those grocery store carts for kids that are roughly shaped like race cars and have plastic steering wheels in them. When I take my kids to the store, I put them in that little cart and they hold the plastic wheel. They love that wheel. Why? Because it makes them feel like they have power. It gives them the illusion that they're in control. They turn the wheel left, and I turn the cart left. They turn the wheel right, and I turn the cart right. They love it. Their eyes light up.

But it's an illusion. I'm only humoring them. Eventually, we need to get down to the business of getting the grocery shopping done. At some point, they try to turn right into the candy aisle, and the cart keeps going straight. They look up at me with disappointment, bewilderment, and dismay, as if to say, "Dad, you tricked us. You gave us this wheel, and it doesn't work. If we could trade you in for a new dad, we would."

The thing is, I've felt that way at work before. I imagine that you have too. I've had times when I wanted to say, "Hey, you gave me this steering wheel, but when I turn it, nothing happens. I try to make changes, but they don't happen. I make decisions, but they don't move the organization." You don't have to respond with apathy. There's another option. And it starts with recognizing that authority is not the same thing as leadership.

Here's what I want to convince you of: The steering wheel—your steering wheel—does work; it just doesn't work based on authority.

We've been taught that leadership is about using the gun of authority. Leaders pull out the gun of authority and say, "If you don't do what I say, then I'll fire you or I'll make life miserable for you." But leaders who leverage authority to get things done aren't great leaders. The greatest leaders leverage influence . . . even when they're in charge.

No one gave Dr. Martin Luther King Jr. authority to lead the Civil Rights Movement. He leveraged his influence to lead the movement. With no official authority, Nelson Mandela leveraged influence to end apartheid in South Africa. And when Mahatma Gandhi led a revolution that changed the nation of India, he did so through influence, not by authority.

NOTES

DISCUSS

Discuss what you just watched by answering the following questions.

1. In thinking about your past, where have you learned the myth that authority and leadership always go hand in hand?

2. Consider someone who had influence in your life even though they didn't have authority over you. What was it about that person that made them influential?

3. In what area of life do you have a lot of authority? In what ways is that authority a positive influence on your leadership? In what ways might it be a negative influence?

4. Think about a time when you had responsibility without authority. What challenges did that create? How much frustration did you experience?

5. As you reflect on that time when you had responsibility without authority, do you think you could have done anything differently to increase your effectiveness and decrease your frustration? Why or why not?

CHALLENGE

Complete this exercise on your own. Take up to fifteen minutes. First, in the space below, write down an area of your life in which you would like to grow in leadership.

On the continuums below, indicate to what degree your leadership in the area you just noted is based on authority or influence (1 = least, 10 = most).

Authority:

| 1 | 2 | 3 | 4 | 5 | 6 | 7 | 8 | 9 | 10 |

Influence:

| 1 | 2 | 3 | 4 | 5 | 6 | 7 | 8 | 9 | 10 |

There's nothing wrong with positional authority. In fact, sometimes it's absolutely essential. But having authority doesn't mean you don't need to cultivate influence. How might your leadership in this area of life look different if you were able to dial up your influence over the people you lead? Write down some thoughts in the space below.

CLOSE

Authority doesn't drive the car of leadership, but influence can. Whether you're an intern, a mid-level manager, or the one in charge, I hope you and your group can learn together how to cultivate more influence so you become the leaders you've always wanted to be. As you close, pray as a group about any issues addressed in this session.

PERSONAL STUDY

During the group time for this week, you explored how leadership is not synonymous with authority. While authority provides control, true leadership relies on *influence*, not power. Great leaders like Martin Luther King Jr., Nelson Mandela, and Mahatma Gandhi achieved transformative change through influence, not authority. Leadership is about inspiring and guiding others, even without formal power, to create meaningful impact. Keep these ideas in mind as you work through the following activities. If you are reading *How to Lead When You're Not in Charge*, first review chapters 1–3 of the book.

READ

In chapter 1 of the book, "The Oddity of Leadership," I reflect on some of my early desires to lead, starting with a few of my experiences back in grade school. What I ultimately learned—which I want to you to understand—is that you don't need to have a *position* to lead. You can lead simply by cultivating influence. If you have a copy of the book, open it to chapter 1 and answer the following questions to cement these ideas in your mind.

1. When have you felt the most alive while leading? What specific moments or roles in your life made you feel that way?

2. How do you typically respond when you feel like your ideas or contributions are being ignored or undervalued?

3. What are some opportunities to lead that you might have missed because you were waiting for authority or permission to act?

4. How can you begin to cultivate *influence* in your current role—regardless of whether or not you hold a formal leadership position?

5. You have the unique opportunity to create "an oasis of excellence" right where you are. How do you sense that God is leading you in this area?

For Further Study: Watch Simon Sinek's talk, "Why Good Leaders Make You Feel Safe" (11:56), at Ted.com. Record some of your thoughts after watching the video.

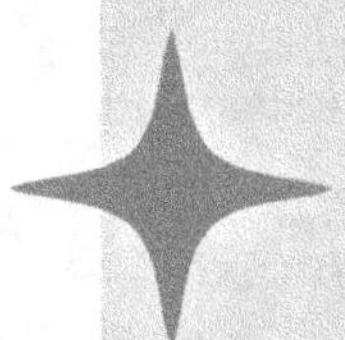

RESPOND

The New Testament is full of great examples of leaders. Matthew tells a story in his Gospel in which Jesus describes for his disciples what is required of a leader in God's kingdom. It happens as the group is walking along the road one day. Read the following Scripture passage and answer the questions that follow.

20 Then the mother of Zebedee's sons came to Jesus with her sons and, kneeling down, asked a favor of him.

21 "What is it you want?" he asked.

She said, "Grant that one of these two sons of mine may sit at your right and the other at your left in your kingdom."

22 "You don't know what you are asking," Jesus said to them. "Can you drink the cup I am going to drink?"

"We can," they answered.

23 Jesus said to them, "You will indeed drink from my cup, but to sit at my right or left is not for me to grant. These places belong to those for whom they have been prepared by my Father."

24 When the ten heard about this, they were indignant with the two brothers. 25 Jesus called them together and said, "You know that the rulers of the Gentiles lord it over them, and their high officials exercise authority over them. 26 Not so with you. Instead, whoever wants to become great among you must be your servant, 27 and whoever wants to be first must be your slave—28 just as the Son of Man did not come to be served, but to serve, and to give his life as a ransom for many."

Matthew 20:20–28

1. The "mother of Zebedee's sons" (verse 20) refers to the disciples James and John. What was her attitude toward leadership?

2. What was her specific question to Jesus? Why do you think she made this request?

3. What did Jesus mean when he asked, "Can you drink the cup I am going to drink?" (verse 22). What was Jesus saying about leadership and sacrifice?

4. How did Jesus go on to contrast the leadership of the Gentile rulers with the kind of leadership he calls his followers to embody in God's kingdom?

5. How does the example of Jesus, who "did not come to be served, but to serve, and to give his life as a ransom for many" (verse 28), influence your approach to leadership?

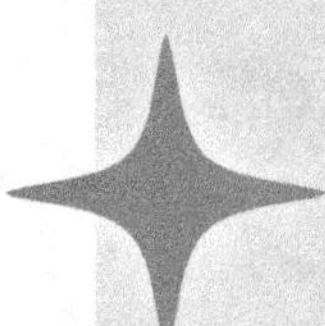

REFLECT

Take a few minutes to review the notes you took during your group time and the answers you wrote down in the previous two personal studies. Use the following questions to reflect on everything you've covered during this first session.

1. When do you first remember wanting to be a leader? What was the situation?

2. When you think about your current roles, to what extent are you finding your identity in the authority or positions you've been given?

3. Is there an area of your life in which you're currently waiting to be given authority? If so, what would it look like for you to build influence in that area?

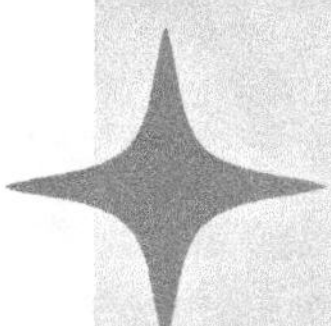

CATCH UP AND READ AHEAD

Connect with a fellow group member this week and discuss some of the key insights from this session. Use any of the following prompts to help guide your discussion.

- How would you define the difference between influence and authority?
- Do you see an area of your life where Jesus would challenge authority? If so, what is that area—and do you feel called to challenge it?
- What are some practical steps you could take this week to shift from a passive to an active leadership mindset?
- How can understanding your strengths and values impact the way you lead? What could your group do to help your understanding?
- What steps can you take this week to develop more self-awareness as a leader? How can your group members support you in doing so?

Use this time to go back and complete any questions from this week you weren't able to finish. Make a note of any revelations you've had or personal insights you've gained.

Read chapter 4 in *How to Lead When You're Not in Charge* before the next group gathering.

WEEK 2
AT A GLANCE

This Week's Reading: Chapter 4 in *How to Lead When You're Not in Charge*

Group Meeting: Read the Overview and Connect with the group (page 16)

Watch the video and take notes (pages 16–18)

Discuss the questions that follow (page 19)

Respond to the teaching and Close (page 20)

Personal Study:

Study 1   Read and answer questions on chapter 4 (pages 22–23)

Study 2   Respond to a related passage from the Bible (pages 24–25)

Study 3   Reflect on what you've studied this week (page 26)

Catch Up and Read Ahead   Connect with someone in your group during the week

(before week 3 group meeting)   Complete any unfinished studies (page 27)

Next Week's Reading   Chapter 5 in *How to Lead When You're Not in Charge*

LEAD YOURSELF

Nothing so conclusively proves a man's ability to lead others as what he does on a day-to-day basis to lead himself.

TOM WATSON

OVERVIEW

In organizations, no one is actually in charge of everything, but all of us are in charge of something. The first and foremost responsibility that is fully under your care is yourself. You are in charge of you. You are in charge of your attitude, your development, and your growth. The sooner you take responsibility for yourself, the sooner you can begin leading yourself well. When you lead yourself well, you will ensure that you will always be well led.

CONNECT

Go around the group and explain how you would finish the following statement: "I will be well led when ____."

WATCH

Watch the video for this session. A summary is provided for your benefit as well as space to take additional notes.

SUMMARY

None of us has all of the authority we want or need. That doesn't mean we can't lead from the spot we're currently in. Most people who think about leading when they're not in charge see a common obstacle: their bosses. These are the kinds of things they say:

"My boss will never go for that."

"She won't listen to me."

"He's not willing to change."

But even if you work for a bad leader, it's not an excuse. Whatever your situation, you have the opportunity to learn from it and become a better leader. But to do so, you'll have to be intentional about practicing the first of four behaviors we're going to talk about over the next four sessions.

Back when my son, Jake, was in preschool, I used to come home and ask him how his day was. But that approach didn't work so well—even when he was a toddler.

I'd ask, "Hey, buddy, how was school?"

He'd say, "Fine."

If I asked my daughter, she'd never stop talking about every small detail of her day. But Jake only gave me one-word answers. So one day I changed my approach. Instead of asking him how school was, I asked him what he learned that day. And then he dropped a truth bomb, right there in our kitchen.

He said, "I learned I'm in charge of me."

At first, I thought, *Who is teaching him this garbage?* But the more I thought about it, the more I realized he was right. Jake's teacher can't make him clean up after himself. She can't keep him from hitting another kid for name-calling. It's up to Jake to regulate himself.

We're no different. Here's the truth you need to know: *Your boss isn't in charge of you; you're in charge of you.* That's why the first behavior to cultivate influence is: Lead Yourself.

If you want to create a game plan for leading yourself well, you need to do three things:

1. MODEL FOLLOWERSHIP

Do you know how to follow well? Does the team you're a part of know that you're following well? If not, you're probably not leading yourself well. Your moral authority is more important than your positional authority. And nothing destroys your moral authority like undermining the person you're supposed to be following—even if that person is a bad leader.

Good self-leadership—even when you're being led poorly—creates influence. It demonstrates to the people around you who you are. It earns trust and admiration. It prepares you for future leadership.

2. MONITOR YOUR HEART AND BEHAVIOR

If you ask people whether it's easier to monitor their behavior or their heart, most people will say their behavior. That's because behavior is tangible. It's measurable. The heart is a bit of a mystery.

In truth, both your heart and your behavior are difficult to monitor. To keep track of your heart, you have to constantly check your motives and feelings before God. King David wrote:

Test me, Lord, and try meexamine my heart and my mind (Psalm 26:2).

That's the attitude we have to cultivate in ourselves if we want to monitor our hearts.

When it comes to monitoring our behavior, the people around us are an invaluable resource. It's not easy to do, but you can increase your awareness of your behavior and take practical steps to change negative behavior by leaning into the people around you. These people orbiting your world—coworkers, friends, and even family—can help you become a better leader. Ask them simple questions like:

- What do I do to inspire you?
- What do I do that bothers you?
- What are my blind spots?

The truths that the answers to those questions reveal may be uncomfortable, but they'll equip you to lead yourself well.

3. MAKE A PLAN

If you want to grow as a leader, you have to figure out your desired leadership destination and make a plan for how to get there. But don't miss the crucial step that so many people do. It's not enough to know where you want to go. You also need to know where you are right now.

Think about one of those maps in the mall. It doesn't help you to know that the store you're looking for is located at A2 if the map doesn't include that little star that says, "You Are Here."

So, think about where you want to go as a leader. And then think about where you are currently. From there, you'll be able to formulate a plan for moving from A to B.

NOTES

DISCUSS

Discuss what you just watched by answering the following questions.

1. During the video, I said, "Your first responsibility as leader is to start leading yourself well." To what extent is this a new idea to you? Do you find it comforting, challenging, or both? Why?

2. Are you currently sacrificing your moral authority by not doing a good job of modeling followership? If so, what is one thing you can do right away to begin to follow your boss or leader well?

3. What are some things you currently do to monitor your heart and behaviors? What can you do to up your game in each area? Who can help you by answering the question, "What is it like to be on the other side of me?"

4. Read Psalm 26:2. What would it look like for you to invite God to examine your heart and mind? What is standing in the way of you extending the invitation?

5. What are some ways that you can brainstorm together as a group about how to determine your self-leadership status so you can then make a plan to move forward?

CHALLENGE

Complete this exercise on your own. Take up to fifteen minutes.

Use the table below to make a self-leadership plan.

First, identify where you currently are in terms of your personal health, the health of your social relationships, and your spiritual health. Be specific about behaviors and emotions you see in yourself.

Next, determine how you want to grow in each area. Again, be specific. It's best if your objectives are concrete and measurable.

Finally, identify what actions you can take to move from where you are to where you want to be. Identify how you will hold yourself accountable and how others can help.

Lead Me Plan	Where Am I	Objectives	Execution and Accountability
Self Health			
Social Health			
Spiritual Health			

CLOSE

Do you want to grow as a leader? The good news is that you don't have to wait around for those who lead you—whether they lead you well or poorly—to take action on your behalf. You can take the initiative by leading yourself well. In fact, it's the best first step no matter what your current situation.

There's no trick to leading yourself well. It requires discipline and intentionality. Figure out where you are. Decide where you want to be. And make a plan for how you're going to get there.

As you close, pray as a group about any issues addressed in this session.

PERSONAL STUDY

During group this week, you saw how leadership starts with self-leadership. You are responsible for your attitude, growth, and actions, regardless of your position or boss. So, to lead yourself well, it is important to model followership, monitor your heart, and create a plan for growth. Self-leadership builds trust and influence and prepares you for future leadership opportunities. Think about these ideas as you work through the following activities. If you are reading *How to Lead When You're Not in Charge*, first review chapter 4 of the book.

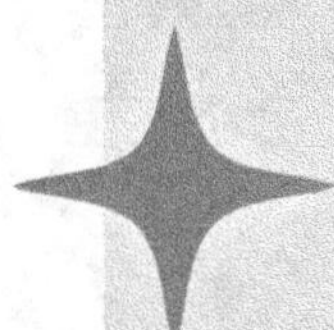

READ

In chapter 4 of the book, "Lead Yourself," I comment on how leadership begins with taking personal responsibility. If you have a copy of the book, open it to that chapter and answer the following questions.

1. How does the idea that "you are in charge of you" challenge the way you currently approach your responsibilities?

2. Have you ever found yourself blaming a boss for your failure to do a job well? How might shifting your focus to leading yourself improve your situation?

3. Out of the three principles of self-leadership, which resonates most with you? How can you apply that particular principle to your current situation?

4. What lessons have you learned from a challenging leadership situation (a "bad leader")? How have these experiences shaped the kind of leader you want to be?

5. Have you ever faced a situation where you had to decide whether to stay in or leave a role? If so, what steps did you take to ensure you made the right decision?

RESPOND

At some point in your life, you *will* be a manager, whether it's leading hundreds of people in an organization or just managing your own time. Read the following parable that Jesus told about a shrewd manager and then answer the questions that follow.

[1] Jesus told his disciples: "There was a rich man whose manager was accused of wasting his possessions. [2] So he called him in and asked him, 'What is this I hear about you? Give an account of your management, because you cannot be manager any longer.'

[3] "The manager said to himself, 'What shall I do now? My master is taking away my job. I'm not strong enough to dig, and I'm ashamed to beg—[4] I know what I'll do so that, when I lose my job here, people will welcome me into their houses.'

[5] "So he called in each one of his master's debtors. He asked the first, 'How much do you owe my master?'

[6] "'Nine hundred gallons of olive oil,' he replied.

"The manager told him, 'Take your bill, sit down quickly, and make it four hundred and fifty.'

[7] "Then he asked the second, 'And how much do you owe?'

"'A thousand bushels of wheat,' he replied.

"He told him, 'Take your bill and make it eight hundred.'

[8] "The master commended the dishonest manager because he had acted shrewdly. For the people of this world are more shrewd in dealing with their own kind than are the people of the light. [9] I tell you, use worldly wealth to gain friends for yourselves, so that when it is gone, you will be welcomed into eternal dwellings.

[10] "Whoever can be trusted with very little can also be trusted with much, and whoever is dishonest with very little will also be dishonest with much. [11] So if you have not been trustworthy in handling worldly wealth, who will trust you with true riches? [12] And if you have not been trustworthy with someone else's property, who will give you property of your own?"

Luke 16:1–12

1. What was the shrewd manager's plan when he learned his master was firing him?

2. Why did the rich master commend the shrewd manager for this plan?

3. How would you describe the kind of leadership the shrewd manager demonstrated in this parable? Who was he leading—and how was he leading?

4. Where you base your trust is important. How do you think the rich master could have avoided this situation with his manager?

5. Jesus commends the manager not for his dishonesty but for his cleverness in devising a plan for his future. What does this say about the importance of having a plan for your leadership—knowing where you are and where you ultimately want to be?

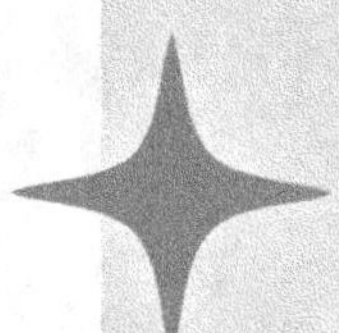

REFLECT

Take a few minutes to review the notes you took during your group time and the answers you wrote down in the previous two personal studies. Use the following questions to reflect on everything you've covered during this second session.

1. In what area of your life is most of your leadership time and energy currently focused?

2. On a scale of 1 ("not very") to 10 ("extremely"), how effectively do you think you are leading in that area?

| 1 | 2 | 3 | 4 | 5 | 6 | 7 | 8 | 9 | 10 |

What are some ways you might better steward yourself to better steward others?

3. Is there someone in your life you could trust to provide you with honest, helpful feedback in the role you just mentioned? (If so, seek out that person's evaluation and jot down some of his or her comments.)

Spend some time praying that God will show you how you can be more trustworthy with the resources and authority he has entrusted to you.

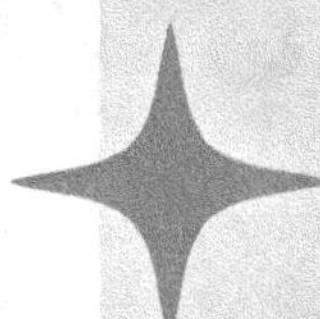

CATCH UP AND READ AHEAD

Connect with a fellow group member and discuss some of the key insights from this session. Use any of the following prompts to help guide your discussion.

- Where do you see the principle of self-leadership applying to your life?
- Where do you particularly want to see growth as a self-leader?
- What does a bad or ineffective leader look like to you? What traits about that kind of leadership do you most want to avoid?
- What did you find most interesting about the parable of the shrewd manager? How did the shrewd manager model self-leadership?
- How have you benefitted from the honest feedback others have provided when it comes to increasing awareness of your behaviors?

Use this time to go back and complete any questions from this week you weren't able to finish. Make a note of any revelations you've had or personal insights you've gained.

Read chapter 5 in *How to Lead When You're Not in Charge* before the next group gathering.

WEEK 3
AT A GLANCE

This Week's Reading:	Chapter 5 in *How to Lead When You're Not in Charge*
Group Meeting:	Read the Overview and Connect with the group (page 30)
	Watch the video and take notes (pages 30–32)
	Discuss the questions that follow (page 33)
	Respond to the teaching and Close (page 34)
Personal Study:	
Study 1	Read and answer questions on chapter 5 (pages 36–37)
Study 2	Respond to a related passage from the Bible (pages 38–39)
Study 3	Reflect on what you've studied this week (page 40)
Catch Up and Read Ahead	Connect with someone in your group during the week
(before week 4 group meeting)	Complete any unfinished studies (page 41)
Next Week's Reading	Chapter 6 in *How to Lead When You're Not in Charge*

CHOOSE POSITIVITY

We see the world, not as it is, but as we are—or as we're conditioned to see it.

STEPHEN COVEY

OVERVIEW

No matter what position you're in, the greatest thing you bring to your team is not your education, experience, or talent but your *energy* (or *attitude*). A positive, can-do, forward-thinking, hope-filled attitude covers a multitude of leadership shortcomings. Great organizations don't just have the best ideas. Great organizations are filled with people giving their best to the same idea. The attitude you have today is completely under your control. Choose wisely.

CONNECT

Discuss whether you tend to see the glass as half full or half empty. Do you think that tendency is your natural temperament, or did you learn it?

WATCH

Watch the video for this session. A summary is provided for your benefit as well as space to take additional notes.

SUMMARY

There's a story told that Sir Edmund Hillary and Tenzing Norgay—the first people to summit Mount Everest—didn't know they'd reached the summit of the tallest mountain on Earth until they looked around and realized there was no ground anywhere in sight higher than where they stood.

Position gives you perspective. It affects how you see the world around you. It affects how you see your organization. If you're an intern, you have a different perspective than a manager who's somewhere in the middle of the organization. And if you're a manager, you have a different perspective than the CEO.

How you see things is incredibly important. Perspective is *everything*. What's your perspective in your organization? However you answer that question, I want to make a recommendation:

Elevate your perspective above where it currently is.

Decide to see things more broadly. Choose to have a panoptic view. *Panoptic* just means "showing the whole at once." Think of a 360-degree panoramic photograph. It can show you everything in a landscape in a single shot—more than what your eyes can see.

To help you see the power of this kind of perspective, let's take a look at what I call the Panoptic Pyramid.

The top of the pyramid represents your view—of the world, of your relationships, of your organization. It's limited. If you want to broaden your view, it will require trust in God and hope for the future.

Trust that where you are right now is exactly where God wants you. It's where you're supposed to be. If you choose to trust, it will broaden your perspective. You may stop seeing where you are as a burden or a barrier and begin to see it as an opportunity. And that could change everything.

Your choice to trust doesn't stand on its own. It's coupled with hope for a better future. This isn't your final job. It's not your final role. You know where you want to go, and you've made a plan for how to get there. But it will take time.

Trust and hope are vital because they allow you to adopt the second behavior that is key to growing in your leadership. If you decide to trust and hope, you'll begin to choose positivity.

Positivity is powerful. It's not a personality trait. It's not about being a positive person versus being a negative person . . . or even a realistic person. It's not about seeing the glass as half full instead of half empty. It's the outflow of a broader perspective.

You can choose positivity. That choice is rooted in trust, and it sees hope for the future.

Choosing positivity changes three things:

1. ENERGY

Your posture of positivity is the most powerful tool in your arsenal. It's deciding that no matter what happens today, you will bring a hope-filled, positive energy. And you don't have to be in charge to bring that energy to your team. One person can change the climate of an entire team—maybe even an entire organization.

2. HUMILITY

Humility determines how you buy into an organization's mission and strategy. How do you handle the decisions that are handed to you that you weren't able to weigh in on? How you choose to manage those situations is determined by your attitude. When you're humble, you can take an idea you don't even believe in and make it work.

3. UNITY

Unity is the idea that *we* is greater than *me*. When you choose positivity, it becomes natural to live out unity, to put the team or organization ahead of yourself. That's huge because that's what great leaders do. They use their authority for the benefit of the people around them. So, learning to live in unity before you have authority cultivates influence and prepares you to lead well in the future.

You can choose positivity today. It just requires broadening your perspective. And if you do so, it will affect your energy, your humility, and your ability to unify your team.

NOTES

DISCUSS

Discuss what you just watched by answering the following questions.

1. Do you ever feel buried so deeply in your organization that you can't see down the road from the position you're in? If so, what have you done to cope with or manage that experience?

2. The panoptic view is the ability to elevate yourself to see beyond your position. What would change about your attitude if you could elevate the view you currently have of your position in your organization?

3. Which of the following do you need to dial up in your work life—energy, humility, or unity? What do you think your deficit in that area may be costing you or your organization?

4. When you *weigh in*, you're more likely to *buy in*. How does someone choose to buy into a decision they did not get to weigh in on?

5. On a scale of 1 ("hardly any") to 10 ("very robust"), how much trust do you have that where you're currently sitting is where you're meant to be?

1	2	3	4	5	6	7	8	9	10

If you answered 7 or higher, to what do you attribute your positivity? If you answered 3 or lower, how much hope do you have for a better future?

CHALLENGE

Complete this exercise on your own. Take up to fifteen minutes.

In the space below, write down some ideas about a better future you might hope for. (Note: You might wish to use the self health, social health, and spiritual health objectives you created last week to guide your imagination.)

Now think about your answer to question 4 in the Group Discussion. What is one thing you can do this week to increase your trust in God?

CLOSE

First Peter 5:6 says, "Humble yourselves, therefore, under God's mighty hand, that he may lift you up in due time." This little verse is simple, but it offers a lot of clarity. It says that your job isn't to lift yourself up. That's up to God, so trust him to do what you can't.

Your job is to practice humility. And when you do that—when you trust God and hope for a better future—you will be able to choose positivity. And that will prepare you for the better future God has planned for you.

As you close, pray as a group about any issues addressed in this session.

PERSONAL STUDY

During this week's group time, you discussed how perspective shapes the way you view the world. You can elevate your perspective by choosing to see things more broadly and trusting that God has put you exactly where he wants you to be for this moment. If you do this, you will embrace positivity, which will have a direct impact on your *energy, humility,* and *unity* with others. Keep these ideas in mind as you work through the following activities. If you are reading *How to Lead When You're Not in Charge,* first review chapter 5 of the book.

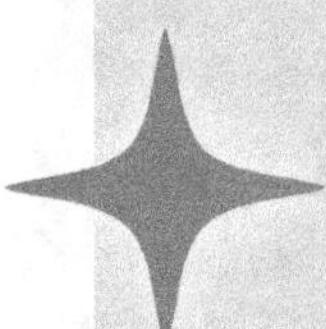

READ

In chapter 5 of the book, "Choose Positivity," I discuss how the perspective you adopt in your current role will shape how you see challenges and opportunities. If you have a copy of the book, open it to that chapter and answer the following questions.

1. In the chapter, I write, "One of the greatest differences in the way each of us sees the world is in how we define the word *vacation*." What is your perspective on what makes a great vacation? How is that perspective different from others in your life?

2. What does it look like for you personally to have a *panoptic* view? How does such a perspective change the way you approach your responsibilities at work?

3. What you believe about God and how you see the future are critical voices for how you will lead right now. How would you describe your view of God? Do you believe that he can truly accomplish *anything* in your life? Why or why not?

4. How about your view of the future—do you have an outlook more of hope or of despair? How might that outlook be influencing your perspective?

5. Read 1 Peter 5:6. What roles does this verse assign to you and God? How is humility a factor in how you view your job, your calling, and your life?

For Further Study: Search online for the white papers "What Drives Employee Engagement and Why It Matters" or "Emotional Drivers of Employee Engagement" from the Dale Carnegie Institute. Record some of your thoughts after reading either of these papers.

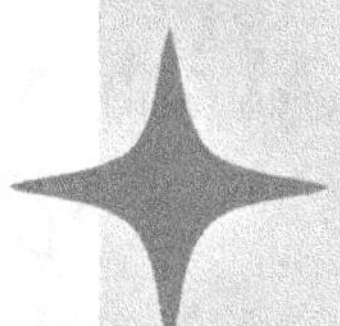

RESPOND

The word *panoptic* comes from the Greek word *pan* (meaning "all, every, whole") and *optikos* (meaning "sight" or "vision")—thus, as we've discussed, one that "shows the whole at once." The apostle Paul had such a panoptic lens in his role as a leader. Read his following words to the church in Philippi and then answer the questions that follow.

[12] Now I want you to know, brothers and sisters, that what has happened to me has actually served to advance the gospel. [13] As a result, it has become clear throughout the whole palace guard and to everyone else that I am in chains for Christ. [14] And because of my chains, most of the brothers and sisters have become confident in the Lord and dare all the more to proclaim the gospel without fear.

[15] It is true that some preach Christ out of envy and rivalry, but others out of goodwill. [16] The latter do so out of love, knowing that I am put here for the defense of the gospel. [17] The former preach Christ out of selfish ambition, not sincerely, supposing that they can stir up trouble for me while I am in chains. [18] But what does it matter? The important thing is that in every way, whether from false motives or true, Christ is preached. And because of this I rejoice.

Yes, and I will continue to rejoice, [19] for I know that through your prayers and God's provision of the Spirit of Jesus Christ what has happened to me will turn out for my deliverance. [20] I eagerly expect and hope that I will in no way be ashamed, but will have sufficient courage so that now as always Christ will be exalted in my body, whether by life or by death. [21] For to me, to live is Christ and to die is gain. [22] If I am to go on living in the body, this will mean fruitful labor for me. Yet what shall I choose? I do not know! [23] I am torn between the two: I desire to depart and be with Christ, which is better by far; [24] but it is more necessary for you that I remain in the body. [25] Convinced of this, I know that I will remain, and I will continue with all of you for your progress and joy in the faith, [26] so that through my being with you again your boasting in Christ Jesus will abound on account of me.

Philippians 1:12–26

1. How does Paul demonstrate that he has panoptic perspective?

2. What did Paul do while he was in prison? How did he demonstrate leadership to the church in Philippi even though he was "in chains for Christ" (verse 13)?

3. What was the only thing that mattered to Paul when it came to how the gospel was preached? How is this an example of humility?

4. What was Paul's perspective on the size of his God? What was his perspective on his future— even though he was currently sitting in a dank prison cell?

5. Paul clearly had a mind fixed on eternity. What is a specific area in your life where an eternal perspective would help you to see your situation differently?

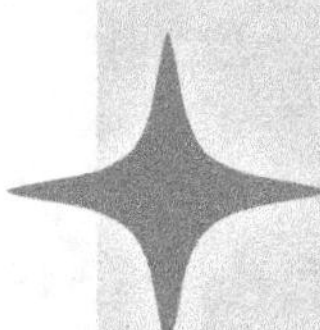

REFLECT

Take a few minutes to review the notes you took during your group time and the answers you wrote down in the previous two personal studies. Use the following questions to reflect on everything you've covered during this third session.

1. Do you tend to be pessimistic or optimistic? There may be no changing your gut reaction to circumstances, but if you tend toward pessimism, how might you begin training your mind toward a more positive viewpoint after initial negativity? And if you tend toward optimism, do you see any possible complications with that approach?

2. Think about the Panoptic Pyramid. What do you find most challenging: maintaining energy in your attitude, having humility toward your authority, or remaining in unity with your associates? Why do you think that is so?

3. Overall, as you reflect on what you've learned this week, what obstacles (if any) stand in the way of you fully trusting God and hoping in the future?

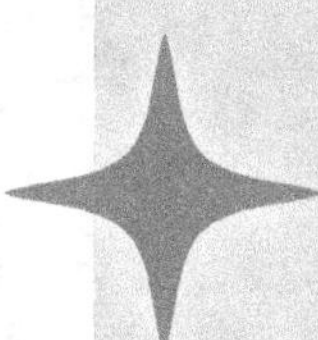

CATCH UP AND READ AHEAD

Connect with a fellow group member and discuss some of the key insights from this session. Use any of the following prompts to help guide your discussion.

- Where are you feeling stuck in your organization? What have you done so far to cope with or manage that experience?
- What insights did you gain this week about your view of God?
- What stood out to you about Paul's perspective in Philippians 1:12–26? Why did that especially stand out to you?
- What would be the benefit of adopting an attitude of positivity when it comes to the energy and drive you demonstrate at work?
- What challenges did you identify when it comes to demonstrating humility in your role or in being united with your associates? What are you choosing to do to address those challenges?

Use this time to go back and complete any of the study and reflection questions from previous days that you weren't able to finish. Make a note below of any revelations you've had and reflect on any growth or personal insights you've gained.

Read chapter 6 in *How to Lead When You're Not in Charge* before the next group gathering.

WEEK 4
AT A GLANCE

This Week's Reading:	Chapter 6 in *How to Lead When You're Not in Charge*
Group Meeting:	Read the Overview and Connect with the group (page 44)
	Watch the video and take notes (pages 44–46)
	Discuss the questions that follow (page 47)
	Respond to the teaching and Close (pages 48–49)
Personal Study:	
Study 1	Read and answer questions on chapter 6 (pages 52–53)
Study 2	Respond to a related passage from the Bible (pages 54–55)
Study 3	Reflect on what you've studied this week (page 56)
Catch Up and Read Ahead	Connect with someone in your group during the week
(before week 5 group meeting)	Complete any unfinished studies (page 57)
Next Week's Reading	Chapter 7 in *How to Lead When You're Not in Charge*

THINK CRITICALLY

You have to decide what your highest priorities are and have the courage—pleasantly, smilingly, unapologetically—to say no to other things. And the way you do that is by having a bigger "yes" burning inside.

CHRIS MCCHESNEY

OVERVIEW

Critical thinking is a skill worth spending time to develop. By being fully present in relationships and environments, critical thinkers notice things, question things, and connect things. They're not content with the status quo but are constantly trying to make it better. However, the line between thinking critically and being critical is razor thin. Although learning to think critically is a skill, being critical is a snare to avoid for anyone looking to cultivate the influence needed to lead well.

CONNECT

Discuss whether you tend to focus on the big picture or the fine details. How does that influence your effectiveness as a leader? How does it help or hinder you as an employee?

WATCH

Watch the video for this session. A summary is provided for your benefit as well as space to take additional notes.

SUMMARY

Fill in the blank: There are two kinds of people in the world—positive and ________________.

If you said "negative," maybe you're mislabeling people. There aren't as many "negative" people as there are "realistic" people.

The last session was about choosing positivity. For some people, that comes naturally. For others, it's annoying. Maybe that's you. If you roll your eyes when you hear the song "Everything Is Awesome" from *The Lego Movie*, that doesn't mean you're negative. It probably means you tend to see how things can be improved instead of how they're already great.

Over the past two sessions, you've explored what it looks like to lead yourself and choose positivity. But doing those two things isn't enough to make you a great leader. You also have to learn to *think critically*.

Those first two behaviors—leading yourself and choosing positivity—have mostly to do with what's going on inside of you. They have to do with your thoughts and emotions. And because they're internal, changing them can be tricky. They involve changes to your perspective and your behavior. They usually require faking it until you make it.

But thinking critically is a skill. Even if it doesn't come naturally to you, even if you'd rather just sing "Everything Is Awesome," you can train yourself to do it. In fact, you need to develop critical thinking skills if you want to grow because *every good leader is also a critical thinker.*

Critical thinkers:

- Connect things
- Notice things
- Question things

In other words, they're able to see strategic connections, pick up on little details that others miss, and demonstrate the kind of curiosity that causes them to ask questions others fail to ask. And those skills produce an insatiable appetite to make things better.

So, how do you up your critical thinking game? Developing those mental muscles requires four significant adjustments:

I. STOP THINKING LIKE AN EMPLOYEE. START THINKING LIKE AN OWNER.

An owner is directly invested in the outcome of the organization and behaves accordingly. An owner takes initiative. An owner does the little things that matter. When you think like an owner, even when you're not one, it grows your influence and prepares you for future leadership.

2. STOP STACKING MEETINGS. START SCHEDULING MEETINGS.

Rushing from one meeting to the next may feel efficient, but it's not. It may be applauded in your organization, but it's not the best way to work. Emphasize quality over quantity. Leave space between meetings so you can debrief what just happened and prepare for what's next. If you want to be a critical thinker, you have to give yourself time to think.

3. STOP BEING CRITICAL. START THINKING CRITICALLY.

Critical *people* are cynical and negative. Critical *thinkers* bring value and ideas. Motive makes all the difference. Critical thinkers aren't out to just point out problems. They're motivated by love. They want to help people and organizations change for the better.

4. STOP GIVING A GRADE. START LENDING A HAND.

In John 13:1–17, we read how Jesus washed the disciples' feet during the Last Supper. In that humble act, he modeled for us what it looks like to lend a hand instead of giving a grade. The disciples had too many shortcomings to list here. But Jesus didn't hand out grades. He didn't make a list of all the ways they were inadequate. He provided them the help they needed. What would it look like for you to lend others a hand? What would it look like to bring ideas with the motive to help others grow?

You can choose to bring value to others as you harness and hone the skill of thinking critically.

NOTES

DISCUSS

Discuss what you just watched by answering the following questions.

1. What is the difference between a *negative* person and a *realistic* person? What assets and perspective would a realistic person bring into a situation?

2. In the video, I stated that critical thinkers question things, notice things, and connect things. Which, if any, of these qualities are strengths for you? Which are weaknesses?

3. What are some ways your behavior might change if you stopped thinking like an employee and started thinking like an owner? Do you think those changes would be worth the effort? Why or why not?

4. Do you stack meetings? If so, what is one thing you can do this week to schedule time and space to think and to use that time well?

5. Are you currently being critical instead of thinking critically? If so, what can you do to realign your motives so that you're *for* the people you work with?

CHALLENGE

Complete this exercise on your own. Take up to fifteen minutes.

In the space below, write down three practical things you can do in each category that would help you improve your critical thinking.

The BL lines below should be fill-in lines for the reader to use to write. Should these be bllm or a different coding?

I can stop thinking like an employee and start thinking like an owner by . . .

- ____
- ____
- ____

I can stop stacking meetings and start scheduling meetings by . . .

- ____
- ____
- ____

I can stop being critical and start thinking critically by . . .

- ____
- ____
- ____

I can stop giving a grade and start lending a hand by . . .

- ____
- ____
- ____

Now pick one option from each category and begin to practice it this week. Ask your group to offer encouragement and hold you accountable.

CLOSE

Become a critical thinker. Become known as a problem solver in your organization. As you work on developing your critical thinking skills, keep one image front of mind: Jesus on his knees, towel in hand, washing the filthy feet of his closest followers. That image is counterintuitive. But it's one of the most profound things Jesus taught us about what it looks like to lead when you're not in charge.

As you close, pray as a group about any issues addressed in this session.

PERSONAL STUDY

During this week's group time, you looked at why critical thinking is essential for leadership. Critical thinkers connect things, notice things, and question things. They prioritize quality over busyness, focus on solutions over criticism, and offer support instead of judgment. Critical thinking, rooted in love and growth, enhances influence and fosters meaningful change. Keep these ideas in mind as you work through the following activities. If you are reading *How to Lead When You're Not in Charge*, first review chapter 6 of the book.

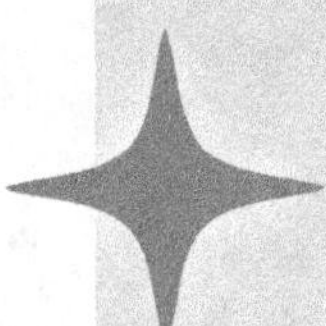

READ

In chapter 6, "Think Critically," I emphasize the importance of balancing positivity with critical thinking in order to become a servant-hearted leader. If you have a copy of the book, open it to that chapter and answer the following questions.

1. How do you personally strike the balance between maintaining a positive outlook and thinking critically—which requires being realistic—in your daily life?

2. Positivity is great, but a *rainbow-puking unicorn* is not. What is an example that comes to mind of when positivity ceased to inspire you and instead made you feel ill?

3. Leaders who are critical thinkers don't just criticize but seek to *learn* from others. How do you make sure your feedback is constructive when you are asking questions and challenging assumptions? How do you show that you have a desire to learn?

4. Leaders who are critical thinkers are also able to connect the feelings people have to the contributing behaviors causing those feelings. Why is this such a necessary skill? What steps do you take to ensure you are considering people's feelings?

5. What role does overcoming challenges play in developing critical thinking?

For Further Study: Search online for the *USA Today* article "Aaron Rodgers' Professor: 'You'll Never Make It in NFL.'" Record some of your thoughts after reading it.

RESPOND

During the Last Supper, Jesus did something that was unthinkable for any leader to do—both back then and today. In the process, he modeled what it meant to be a servant-hearted leader. Read the following passage and then answer the questions that follow.

¹ It was just before the Passover Festival. Jesus knew that the hour had come for him to leave this world and go to the Father. Having loved his own who were in the world, he loved them to the end.

² The evening meal was in progress, and the devil had already prompted Judas, the son of Simon Iscariot, to betray Jesus. ³ Jesus knew that the Father had put all things under his power, and that he had come from God and was returning to God; ⁴ so he got up from the meal, took off his outer clothing, and wrapped a towel around his waist. ⁵ After that, he poured water into a basin and began to wash his disciples' feet, drying them with the towel that was wrapped around him.

⁶ He came to Simon Peter, who said to him, "Lord, are you going to wash my feet?"

⁷ Jesus replied, "You do not realize now what I am doing, but later you will understand."

⁸ "No," said Peter, "you shall never wash my feet."

Jesus answered, "Unless I wash you, you have no part with me."

⁹ "Then, Lord," Simon Peter replied, "not just my feet but my hands and my head as well!"

¹⁰ Jesus answered, "Those who have had a bath need only to wash their feet; their whole body is clean. And you are clean, though not every one of you." ¹¹ For he knew who was going to betray him, and that was why he said not every one was clean.

¹² When he had finished washing their feet, he put on his clothes and returned to his place. "Do you understand what I have done for you?" he asked them. ¹³ "You call me 'Teacher' and 'Lord,' and rightly so, for that is what I am. ¹⁴ Now that I, your Lord and Teacher, have washed your feet, you also should wash one another's feet. ¹⁵ I have

set you an example that you should do as I have done for you. [16] Very truly I tell you, no servant is greater than his master, nor is a messenger greater than the one who sent him. [17] Now that you know these things, you will be blessed if you do them."

John 13:1–17

1. How does John set up this story in verse 1? What is the significance of Jesus spending this dedicated time with his disciples now that "the hour had come"?

2. John writes that Jesus "knew that the Father had put all things under his power" (verse 3). Why do you think John added this detail about Jesus' authority? How does that serve to reinforce just how surprising Jesus' next actions will be?

3. Notice that Jesus even washed the feet of Judas, the disciple who would betray him. What does this add to your understanding about being a servant-hearted leader?

4. How did Peter respond when he saw that Jesus was about to wash his feet? What reason did Jesus provide in verses 15–17 as to why he had done this for them?

5. When you examine Jesus' leadership in this story, what does it reveal about adopting a "towel" mentality as opposed to a "clipboard" state of mind?

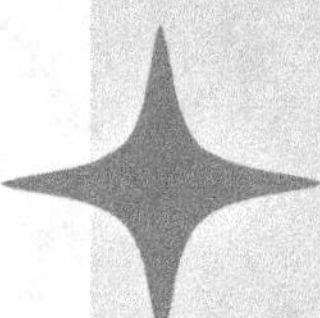

REFLECT

Take a few minutes to review the notes you took during your group time and the answers you wrote down in the previous two personal studies. Use the following questions to reflect on everything you've covered during this fourth session.

1. In what ways do critical people affect your motivation?

2. Critical thinkers connect things, notice things, and question things. Which of those three qualities comes naturally to you? Which takes more effort?

3. Does your current meeting schedule help or hinder your critical thinking? Even if you don't have the power to change the schedule, what adjustments could you make to enhance your critical thinking?

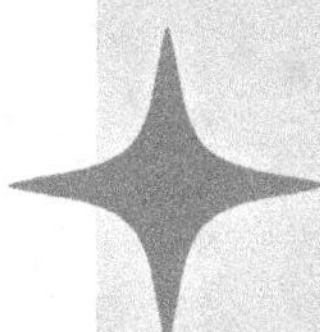

CATCH UP AND
READ AHEAD

Connect with a fellow group member and discuss some of the key insights from this session. Use any of the following prompts to help guide your discussion.

- Which option in the Challenge section did you select for improving your critical thinking? What steps have you taken to progress in that area?
- How are you demonstrating that you want to be a good learner—not just a criticizer— and are open to receiving feedback?
- What do you think is most difficult about connecting the feelings people have to the contributing behaviors causing those feelings?
- What stood out to you in Jesus' example of servant-hearted leadership? How do you think the disciples were changed after that event?
- What does your weekly schedule like? Is there room for you to take time to think critically, connect ideas, read your Bible, and pray?

Use this time to go back and complete any of the study and reflection questions from previous days that you weren't able to finish. Make a note below of any revelations you've had and reflect on any growth or personal insights you've gained.

Read chapter 7 in *How to Lead When You're Not in Charge* before the next group gathering.

WEEK 5
AT A GLANCE

This Week's Reading:	Chapter 7 in *How to Lead When You're Not in Charge*

Group Meeting:

Read the Overview and Connect with the group (page 60)

Watch the video and take notes (pages 60–62)

Discuss the questions that follow (page 63)

Respond to the teaching and Close (page 64)

Personal Study:

Study 1 — Read and answer questions on chapter 7 (pages 66–67)

Study 2 — Respond to a related passage from the Bible (pages 68–70)

Study 3 — Reflect on what you've studied this week (page 71)

Catch Up and Read Ahead
(before week 6 group meeting)

Connect with someone in your group during the week

Complete any unfinished studies (page 72)

Next Week's Reading

Chapters 8–9 in *How to Lead When You're Not in Charge*

REJECT PASSIVITY

You will never passively find what you do not actively pursue.

TIM COOPER

OVERVIEW

Being the boss has its challenges, but being able to call the shots, make decisions, and choose the direction at least gives a semblance of control. Conversely, one of the most common challenges of not being in charge is the lack of perceived control. When you feel out of control, you'll naturally drift toward passivity. Avoiding the trap of sitting on your hands in resignation or throwing your hands up in frustration is crucial in leading when you don't have authority.

CONNECT

Discuss as a group how you usually respond to stress. Is your instinct to retreat and hope everything works out or to take immediate action in order to resolve the problem? What are the advantages to your approach? What are the disadvantages?

WATCH

Watch the video for this session. A summary is provided for your benefit as well as space to take additional notes.

SUMMARY

When I was a college student, one of my good friends got a pickup truck. It was great, except for one thing: Owning a pickup is the kiss of death to your free time. In fact, it's an open invitation to anyone who is moving from their apartment or house to help you haul their stuff across town or even across the state.

One time we were helping a family move their pool table from their old home to their new one. It was a big job. Pool tables are heavy and awkward. But the best part of the job was the seventy-five-year-old grandfather who took it upon himself to act as our foreman. As he watched us move the pool table, he offered a running commentary on everything we were doing wrong— every misstep we made, every wall we scraped.

I'll never forget the piece of advice he offered us again and again in his raspy, cigarette-scarred voice: "Don't let it beat cha!"

There are things in life that want to beat you. Lack of authority is one of those things. When you're not in charge, there is something that wants to get into your heart and your mind and make you unhealthy.

As your authority goes down, the feeling that you lack control goes up. That's dangerous, because the feeling of being out of control pulls us toward passivity. It makes us want to check out. Sometimes, it makes us want to give up.

That brings us to our fourth and final behavior. If you want to cultivate more influence, you have to reject passivity. When you don't have all the authority you want or need, you have to be intentional about rejecting passivity.

When you're not the senior leader, it's easy to be plagued by the "swoop and poop." This is when a team or group of mid-level leaders make a decision and begin to execute on that decision, only to learn later that their boss has changed the game plan. The boss "swoops" in and "poops" on the original idea. It can leave you feeling dejected. It can leave you feeling like you've wasted a lot of time and energy.

The worst thing is what happens next time. The team will be more passive. They'll be more reluctant to make a decision, expend mental energy, or sacrifice their time on the next idea. We're reluctant to give our all if the plan may change.

Over time, that kind of passivity can bake itself into who we are as leaders and as people. So, we have to fight against it. We have to choose to reject passivity if we're going to cultivate influence.

To do that, we have to apply CPR:

CHOOSING

Pick something. It's easy to sit back and wait for others to give you direction and responsibility. No one wants to waste time and effort. But you can choose to pick something up and run with it. What are some problems that come up in meetings over and over again? Don't wait for someone to give you marching orders. Pick up the problem and make it great. Even if your solution isn't perfect, you've done something in an area where nothing was being done. And you've taken a step to reject passivity in yourself.

PLANNING

Put a plan together. When you bring ideas to the table, you cultivate influence even when you don't have authority. If you're in a meeting and a problem comes up in the discussion, and you've thought about that problem and have put together a plan to address it, you are exerting influence. Usually, an idea that has spent time in the oven wins the meeting, even if it's half-baked. If you've put the energy into planning, it means others don't have to.

RESPONDING

Don't just pick a project that you want to tackle. Respond to what your boss cares most about. One of your main responsibilities is to manage the anxieties of the person you work for. To know that, you may have to ask that person, "What do you see in the organization that's bothering you or worrying you?" And then respond to their answer.

If you decide to apply a little CPR to your passivity, it will resuscitate the energy and intentionality in you so that you're better able to cultivate influence now and become the leader you want to be down the road.

NOTES

DISCUSS

Discuss what you just watched by answering the following questions.

1. What are some things that frustrate you the most about not being in charge? How much of your mental and emotional energy do those things currently consume?

2. In the video, I said, "The more out of control I feel, the more likely I am to just sit back in passivity, not doing what I think needs to be done." Do you recognize that tendency in yourself as well? Explain your response.

3. Think about a time when you sat back and waited for the opportunity to lead. What lessons might you have learned sooner if you hadn't been so passive?

4. One role of a person who is not in charge is to manage the anxiety of the boss. What is your boss currently worried or anxious about? What can you do to help with that?

5. Instead of waiting for direction or being hesitant to take on more responsibilities, what can you choose to pick up right now? How can you make a plan to deal with it? What steps can you take to ensure you are responding to what your boss cares about?

CHALLENGE

Complete this exercise on your own. Take up to fifteen minutes.

If you want to reject passivity, it's time to start CPR. Think of a way you can make a difference in your organization. (Maybe this is an issue that's bothering or worrying your boss.) Start the process now by brainstorming a few steps to set a solution in motion.

Choosing: What need, concern, or problem will you pick up and address?

Planning: What is your plan on how to address that need, concern, or problem?

Responding: How does your solution incorporate what your boss cares most about?

CLOSE

My friend Tim Cooper says, "You will never find passively what you do not actively pursue." You won't stumble into influence. You won't bump into leadership or wait your way into it. Don't let the feeling of having little control stop you from finding a way to take the initiative by choosing, planning, and responding to reject passivity.

As you close, pray as a group about any issues addressed in this session.

PERSONAL STUDY

During this week's group time, you saw that even though you might be lacking in authority, you should resist passivity by taking the initiative. You do this through CPR: *Choosing* to tackle problems, *planning* solutions to those problems, and *responding* to your boss's priorities. By overcoming passivity, you will build energy, intentionality, and influence. Keep these ideas in mind as you work through the following activities. If you are reading *How to Lead When You're Not in Charge*, first review chapter 7 of the book.

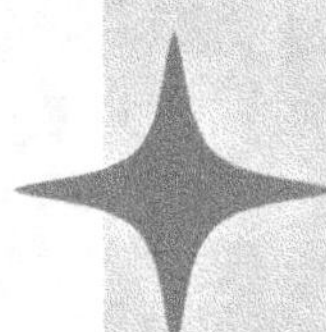

READ

In chapter 7, "Reject Passivity," I encourage you to reject that nagging instinct to *wait* for direction and instead actively seek to take *ownership* of tasks. If you have a copy of the book, open it to that chapter and answer the following questions.

1. Think about the story I tell in this chapter of the man who yelled, "Don't let it beat cha!" as a friend and I moved a pool table. What in your life has served as your rallying cry to not let challenges or obstacles "beat cha"?

2. Think about those situations at work or elsewhere where you lack control. What do you find the most frustrating about those particular situations?

3. What do you think would change if you were the one in control in those situations? What other challenges might you face if you were the one in control?

4. What would it look like for you to remain engaged and proactive in those situations where you are not directly in control? What steps could you take to start doing this?

5. In this chapter I mention some of the *better daily habits* that I started doing to become the kind of leader I wanted to be. Which of your daily habits need some improvement? How would changing some of those habits help move you forward toward your goals?

RESPOND

If there is one person in the Bible who could have allowed his circumstances to beat him down, it was Joseph. He endured trial after trial, yet he stayed resilient and trusted in God. Read the following episode from his life and then answer the questions that follow.

¹ Now Joseph had been taken down to Egypt. Potiphar, an Egyptian who was one of Pharaoh's officials, the captain of the guard, bought him from the Ishmaelites who had taken him there.

² The LORD was with Joseph so that he prospered, and he lived in the house of his Egyptian master. ³ When his master saw that the LORD was with him and that the LORD gave him success in everything he did, ⁴ Joseph found favor in his eyes and became his attendant. Potiphar put him in charge of his household, and he entrusted to his care everything he owned. ⁵ From the time he put him in charge of his household and of all that he owned, the LORD blessed the household of the Egyptian because of Joseph. The blessing of the LORD was on everything Potiphar had, both in the house and in the field. ⁶ So Potiphar left everything he had in Joseph's care; with Joseph in charge, he did not concern himself with anything except the food he ate.

Now Joseph was well-built and handsome, ⁷ and after a while his master's wife took notice of Joseph and said, "Come to bed with me!"

⁸ But he refused. "With me in charge," he told her, "my master does not concern himself with anything in the house; everything he owns he has entrusted to my care. ⁹ No one is greater in this house than I am. My master has withheld nothing from me except you, because you are his wife. How then could I do such a wicked thing and sin against God?" ¹⁰ And though she spoke to Joseph day after day, he refused to go to bed with her or even be with her.

¹¹ One day he went into the house to attend to his duties, and none of the household

servants was inside. [12] She caught him by his cloak and said, "Come to bed with me!" But he left his cloak in her hand and ran out of the house.

[13] When she saw that he had left his cloak in her hand and had run out of the house, [14] she called to her household servants. "Look," she said to them, "this Hebrew has been brought to us to make sport of us! He came in here to sleep with me, but I screamed. [15] When he heard me scream for help, he left his cloak beside me and ran out of the house."

[16] She kept his cloak beside her until his master came home. [17] Then she told him this story: "That Hebrew slave you brought us came to me to make sport of me. [18] But as soon as I screamed for help, he left his cloak beside me and ran out of the house."

[19] When his master heard the story his wife told him, saying, "This is how your slave treated me," he burned with anger. [20] Joseph's master took him and put him in prison, the place where the king's prisoners were confined.

But while Joseph was there in the prison, [21] the LORD was with him; he showed him kindness and granted him favor in the eyes of the prison warden. [22] So the warden put Joseph in charge of all those held in the prison, and he was made responsible for all that was done there. [23] The warden paid no attention to anything under Joseph's care, because the LORD was with Joseph and gave him success in whatever he did.

Genesis 39:1–23

1. Joseph's time in Egypt started well. What was his situation after he was taken into Potiphar's house? How did God show that he was blessing Joseph?

2. How did Joseph act as an owner instead of as an employee in this role? How do you think the story would have gone if Joseph hadn't adopted this mindset?

3. How did Joseph engage in CPR (choosing, planning, responding) in Potiphar's household? Briefly explain how he employed each step.

4. Joseph could have allowed his wrongful conviction to cause him to react with passivity while in prison. But what did he do instead?

5. Where do you feel stuck or powerless this week? How does this story from Joseph's life encourage you to stay in the fight and not let it "beat cha"?

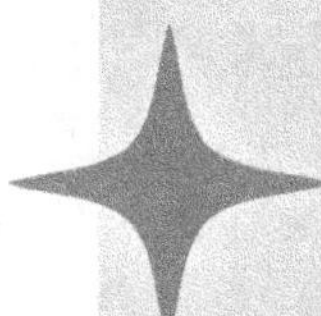

REFLECT

Take a few minutes to review the notes you took during your group time and the answers you wrote down in the previous two personal studies. Use the following questions to reflect on everything you've covered during this fifth session.

1. As you look back on everything you've covered this week, how easy is it for you to drift into passivity? What types of situations cause passivity in you?

2. Are you currently in a period of waiting in some area at work, home, or church? If so, describe the circumstances.

3. If you are currently in a period of waiting, how might God be using this time to prepare you for what comes next?

Spend some time praying that God fosters patience in you while also helping you take action where and when it's appropriate.

CATCH UP AND READ AHEAD

Connect with a fellow group member and discuss some of the key insights from this session. Use any of the following prompts to help guide your discussion.

- What are you currently doing in your role to manage the anxiety of your boss? What could you be doing to better manage that?
- What did you determine that you could do to remain engaged and proactive in those situations where you are not directly in control?
- What did you learn from Joseph's story about the good that can come from choosing to act as an owner instead of an employee in your role?
- What did you learn from Joseph's story about not allowing circumstances outside your control to derail you acting like an owner in your role?
- Do you feel "stuck" somewhere in your life right now? If so, is there something you could do to lead yourself out of that mindset?

Use this time to go back and complete any of the study and reflection questions from previous days that you weren't able to finish. Make a note below of any revelations you've had and reflect on any growth or personal insights you've gained.

Read chapters 8–9 in *How to Lead When You're Not in Charge* before the next group gathering.

WEEK 6
AT A GLANCE

This Week's Reading:	Chapters 8–9 in *How to Lead When You're Not in Charge*
Group Meeting:	Read the Overview and Connect with the group (page 76)
	Watch the video and take notes (pages 76–79)
	Discuss the questions that follow (pages 79–80)
	Respond to the teaching and Close (pages 81–82)
Personal Study:	
Study 1	Read and answer questions on chapters 8–9 (pages 84–85)
Study 2	Respond to a related passage from the Bible (pages 86–88)
Study 3	Reflect on what you've studied this week (page 89)
Wrap Up	Connect with someone in your group during the week
	Complete any unfinished studies (page 90)
Final Reading	Chapter 10 in *How to Lead When You're Not in Charge*

CHALLENGING UP

Leaders search for opportunities for people to exceed their previous levels of performance. They regularly set the bar higher. And the best leaders understand the importance of setting the bar at a level at which people feel they can succeed.

JAMES M. KOUZES AND BARRY Z. POSNER

OVERVIEW

Good leaders have the instinct to do what needs to be done. When they see a problem, they want to fix it. When they find a gap, they want to fill it. And really good leaders find solutions no one else would have thought of. That's great, unless you don't have authority to fix the problem you see *and* the people who have the authority don't see the problem at all. What do you do when solving a problem requires you to challenge the people who have authority over you?

CONNECT

Before you watch the video together, spend a few minutes talking about a time when you saw a solution to a problem even though no one else could see it. What did you do?

WATCH

Watch the video for this session. A summary is provided for your benefit as well as space to take additional notes.

SUMMARY

You've heard of Chick-fil-A, right? If you haven't, it's a chain of restaurants that sells about the best chicken sandwich in the universe. And it's headquartered in Atlanta, Georgia, where I live. So, I get plenty of exposure to Chick-fil-A—both in terms of eating their food and meeting people who work for the corporation.

Some time ago, I met Shane Todd. He's a Chick-fil-A operator. That means he's a franchisee. He owns a Chick-fil-A restaurant. And that puts him in exactly the kind of leadership position we've talked about throughout this study. On the one hand, he's the boss when it comes to running his restaurant and leading his employees. On the other hand, he's not autonomous. Chick-fil-A headquarters has a lot of say in how he operates his business and the quality standards he must meet.

For a couple of years, Shane wanted to add a milkshake to Chick-fil-A's menu. He believed there was customer demand for it. In fact, he'd had many customers specifically ask for the addition of milkshakes.

Shane sat down with his boss, the director of menu strategy for Chick-fil-A. This guy could have squashed Shane's idea as soon as it was expressed. But Shane was very intentional about how he pitched the idea. He made it clear that he would never do anything that was off-brand for the organization. He wasn't interested in launching Chick-fil-A pizza or Buffalo wings. But he was curious about the possibility of introducing a milkshake. Why hadn't that already happened? What was holding the company back from offering an item that customers seemed to want?

Shane began by acknowledging that he didn't know all there was to know about the topic. In fact, there might be factors at play that he wasn't even aware of. He might have some strategic blind spots preventing him from seeing the big picture.

Here's what he learned: Chick-fil-A didn't have anything against milkshakes, specifically. But they did have a big problem with anything that might compromise customers' drive-through experience. If making milkshakes slowed down the drive-through, even a little bit, the ripple effect might create a significant downgrade of the experience for customers. And at Chick-fil-A, customer experience is a sacred cow (pun intended).

This information allowed Shane to challenge the process in a healthy and effective way. He was able to respond, "I hear you. I understand the customer's experience is the most important thing. I don't want to lose any business, but I think this may allow us to expand the business while still staying core to who we are."

And then Shane asked a key question: "Can I try something?" This is so important, because asking for the freedom to experiment in a controlled environment and in a way that won't create dire consequences for the organization is one of the best—and smartest—ways to *challenge up*.

Shane asked for permission to try an experiment for a couple of months. His team would mix up ice cream with chocolate syrup, put whipped cream and a cherry on top, and serve a milkshake. And they'd find a way of doing it without compromising drive-through time.

His boss gave him the go-ahead, and by the end of the agreed-upon time frame for the experiment, his store was selling a couple hundred milkshakes each day. The rest is history. If there's one thing Chick-fil-A is known for, besides their chicken sandwiches, it's their milkshakes.

And here's the thing: If that kind of leading through influence is possible for Shane, it's possible for you.

If you decide to have that courageous conversation by acknowledging your potential blind spots, asserting that you don't want to do anything to compromise the core values of the business, and asking for permission to conduct a short-term, low-risk experiment, you can have more influence than you would ever dream is possible. I really believe that's true.

In the Old Testament, the hero of the book of Esther found herself in the unlikely position of being queen to the king of Persia. It was a role with a tremendous potential for influence . . . and no authority. The king had all of the authority.

When Esther's people, the Hebrews, fell under persecution in Persia, she was asked by her confidante, Mordecai, to use her influence to *challenge up*. This was a risky thing to do because displeasing the king could be fatal. In fact, here's how Esther described the danger to Mordecai:

> "All the king's officials and the people of the royal provinces know that for any man or woman who approaches the king in the inner court without being summoned the king has but one law: that they be put to death unless the king extends the gold scepter to them and spares their lives. But thirty days have passed since I was called to go to the king." (Esther 4:11)

In other words, you didn't visit the king unless the king asked for you. But this is how Mordecai responded to Esther's reluctance to act:

> "For if you remain silent at this time, relief and deliverance for the Jews will arise from another place, but you and your father's family will perish. And who knows but that you have come to your royal position for such a time as this?" (verse 14)

Maybe God put Esther in the position of queen so that she could use her influence on behalf of others. Maybe her role was to make things better for the people around her.

And maybe that's true of you as well. Your opportunity to challenge up probably doesn't come with the risk of execution. But that doesn't mean it isn't scary. Don't let fear stand in your way. Maybe the change you see so clearly, the position you're currently in, the authority you *don't* have, and the influence you *do* have put you in a unique position at just the right time to make things better for the people around you.

NOTES

DISCUSS

Discuss what you just watched by answering the following questions.

1. What value do core organizational vision, goals, strategy, and priorities play in assessing the effectiveness of a particular approach to solving a problem?

2. In what ways can organizational assumptions sometimes get in the way of identifying and executing the best solution to a problem?

3. Have you ever had a subordinate come to you with an out-of-the-box solution to a problem? If so, what obstacles did you have to overcome to be able to openly consider what they had to offer?

4. What role do you think practicing curiosity plays in successfully challenging up?

5. Think about a time when you had an idea of how to solve a problem but no authority to implement that idea. What, if anything, could you have done differently in order to successfully challenge up?

CHALLENGE

Complete this exercise on your own. Take up to fifteen minutes.

Is there currently an opportunity for you to influence your organization by challenging up? If so, on a scale of 1 ("not intimidated at all") to 10 ("scared spitless"), how would rate your fear or worry about challenging those in positions of authority over you?

| 1 | 2 | 3 | 4 | 5 | 6 | 7 | 8 | 9 | 10 |

Why did you give yourself that particular rating? Write your answer in the space below.

What is the worst-case scenario in terms of how your challenge might be received? Write some thoughts in the space below.

Use the following questions to develop strategies for presenting your challenge in the best light possible.

- *How can I acknowledge my potential organizational blind spots? What questions can I ask to better understand the perspective of those who lead me?*

- *How can I communicate that I don't want to do anything to compromise the core values of the organization?*

- *What is a reasonable length of time to conduct a short-term experiment?*

- *What parameters can I establish to ensure the experiment is low risk to the organization?*

CLOSE

Your courage to challenge up may change the future of the organization you find yourself in today. If you figure out a healthy way to challenge those with authority over you, you may be able to affect more change than you ever thought was possible. But it will require you to learn to lead even when you're not in charge.

As you close, pray as a group about any issues addressed in this session. And thank God for how he has used this study to broaden your understanding of leadership as well as grow your relationship with him and with the other members of your group.

PERSONAL STUDY

During the final group time the week, you saw how great leaders influence without authority by "challenging up." They acknowledge blind spots, align their values with those of their boss, and propose low-risk experiments to address problems. Like Esther and Shane Todd, your position and perspective may uniquely equip you to make a meaningful difference. Keep these ideas in mind as you work through the following activities. If you are reading *How to Lead When You're Not in Charge*, first review chapters 8–9 of the book.

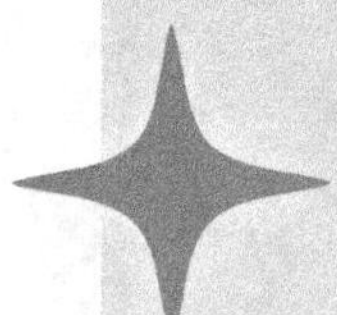

READ

In chapter 8, "Challenging Up," I explore the importance of challenging the status quo with wisdom and communicating your vision in a way that fosters collaboration and trust. In chapter 9, "Breaking Down Challenging Up," I emphasize that challenging up requires building strong relationships, maintaining a humble posture, clearly defining the purpose behind the challenge, and approaching conversations with curiosity and respect. If you have a copy of the book, open it to those chapters and answer the following questions.

1. As you reflect on your own leadership experiences, how have you approached challenging the status quo? How difficult was this for you to do?

2. How did you approach proposing changes in a way that built trust with your boss or manager and avoided making them feel defensive or criticized?

3. How did you ensure your motives were aligned with the greater good of the organization rather than just your own personal gain?

4. Read Philippians 2:3–4. How could this passage help guide you to always keep your boss or manager's interests ahead of your own?

5. We have all had conversations derailed because of a poor approach. What conclusions have you reached about the best way to approach your boss or manager when you want to challenge up and initiate change?

For Further Study: Search online for the *Atlantic* article "How Curt Flood Changed Baseball and Killed His Career in the Process." Record some of your thoughts after reading it.

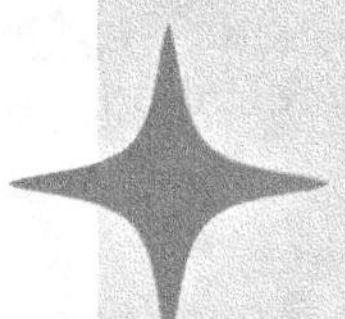

RESPOND

You touched on the story of Esther and Mordecai during this week's group time, but now take some focused time to read the entire account. As you do, consider how Esther and Mordecai "challenged up," and then answer the questions that follow.

[1] When Mordecai learned of all that had been done, he tore his clothes, put on sackcloth and ashes, and went out into the city, wailing loudly and bitterly. [2] But he went only as far as the king's gate, because no one clothed in sackcloth was allowed to enter it. [3] In every province to which the edict and order of the king came, there was great mourning among the Jews, with fasting, weeping and wailing. Many lay in sackcloth and ashes.

[4] When Esther's eunuchs and female attendants came and told her about Mordecai, she was in great distress. She sent clothes for him to put on instead of his sackcloth, but he would not accept them. [5] Then Esther summoned Hathak, one of the king's eunuchs assigned to attend her, and ordered him to find out what was troubling Mordecai and why.

[6] So Hathak went out to Mordecai in the open square of the city in front of the king's gate. [7] Mordecai told him everything that had happened to him, including the exact amount of money Haman had promised to pay into the royal treasury for the destruction of the Jews. [8] He also gave him a copy of the text of the edict for their annihilation, which had been published in Susa, to show to Esther and explain it to her, and he told him to instruct her to go into the king's presence to beg for mercy and plead with him for her people.

[9] Hathak went back and reported to Esther what Mordecai had said. [10] Then she instructed him to say to Mordecai, [11] "All the king's officials and the people of the royal provinces know that for any man or woman who approaches the king in the inner court without being summoned the king has but one law: that they be put to death unless the king extends the gold scepter to them and spares their lives. But thirty days have passed since I was called to go to the king."

¹² When Esther's words were reported to Mordecai, ¹³ he sent back this answer: "Do not think that because you are in the king's house you alone of all the Jews will escape. ¹⁴ For if you remain silent at this time, relief and deliverance for the Jews will arise from another place, but you and your father's family will perish. And who knows but that you have come to your royal position for such a time as this?"

¹⁵ Then Esther sent this reply to Mordecai: ¹⁶ "Go, gather together all the Jews who are in Susa, and fast for me. Do not eat or drink for three days, night or day. I and my attendants will fast as you do. When this is done, I will go to the king, even though it is against the law. And if I perish, I perish."

¹⁷ So Mordecai went away and carried out all of Esther's instructions.

Esther 4:1–17

1. What Mordecai learned "had been done" (verse 1) was an edict issued by the authority of the Persian king to annihilate all the Jews. How did Mordecai respond to this news? How did he advocate for his people?

2. How did Mordecai challenge Esther to work to change this edict? What (quite valid) reservations did Esther have in approaching the king?

3. What does Esther's response reveal she knew about the king? Why was it critical for her to know how the king felt about her before she executed this plan?

4. Esther called for a united fast among the Jews in preparation for this great challenge. Why do you think she did this? What did she realize she needed in this moment?

5. Overall, what were Mordecai and Esther's motives when they sought to challenge authority? How were they strategic in how they approached the issue?

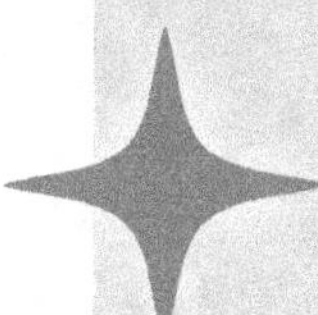

REFLECT

Take a few minutes to review the notes you took during your group time and the answers you wrote down in the previous two personal studies. Use the following questions to reflect on everything you've covered during this sixth session.

1. How comfortable are you with the idea of challenging the people who lead you? If you have room to grow in this area (and most of us do), what are some steps you could take to become more assertive?

2. How easily do you see systems and processes that could be changed to improve results, productivity, or efficiency? Do you think it's possible to acquire or grow this ability, or do you believe it is a trait one is born with?

3. What are some things you currently do to try to see things from the perspective of those who lead you?

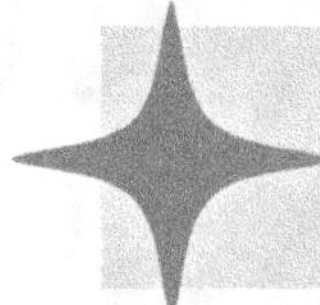

WRAP UP

Connect with a fellow group member and discuss some of the key insights from this session. Use any of the following prompts to help guide your discussion.

- What role does practicing curiosity play in successfully challenging up?
- Is there a situation in your life where you are hesitant to challenge authority? If so, what is causing you to hold back?
- Why is it critical to consider the relationship you have with your boss—how each of you feel about the other—before challenging up?
- What insights did you gain from the story of Esther and Mordecai as it relates to having the right motives when you challenge up?
- How can your fellow group members support you as you finish this study?

Use this time to go back and complete any of the study and reflection questions from previous days that you weren't able to finish. Make a note below of any revelations you've had and reflect on any growth or personal insights you've gained. If you're reading the the book along with this study, read chapter 10.

Finally, discuss with your group what studies you might want to go through next and when you will plan on meeting together again to study God's Word.

LEADER'S GUIDE

You probably have a mental picture of what it will look like to lead—what you'll say and how group members will respond. However, before you get too far into planning, there are some things you should know about leading a small group discussion.

CULTIVATE DISCUSSION

It's easy to assume that a group meeting lives or dies on the quality of your ideas. That's not true. It's the ideas of everyone in the group that make a small group meeting successful. Your role is to create an environment in which people feel safe to share their thoughts. That's how relationships will grow and thrive among your group members.

Here's a basic truth about spiritual growth within the context of community: The study materials aren't as important as the relationships through which those materials take practical shape in the lives of the group members. The more meaningful the relationships, the more meaningful the study. The best materials in the world won't change lives in a sterile environment.

POINT TO THE MATERIAL

A good host creates an environment where people can connect relationally. The host knows when to help guests connect and when to stay out of the way when those connections are happening organically. As a small group leader, sometimes you'll simply read a discussion question and invite everyone to respond. The conversation will take care of itself. At other times you may need to encourage group members to share their ideas. Remember, some of the best insights will come from the people in your group. Go with the flow, but be ready to nudge the conversation in the right direction when necessary.

DEPART FROM THE MATERIAL

We've carefully designed this study for your small group. We've written the materials and designed the questions to elicit the kinds of conversations we think will be most helpful to your group members. But that doesn't mean you should stick rigidly to the materials. Knowing when to depart from them is more art than science, and no one knows more about your group than you do.

The stories, questions, and exercises are here to provide a framework for exploration. But different groups have different chemistries and different motivations. Sometimes the best way to start a small group discussion is to ask, "Does anyone have a personal insight you'd like to share from this week's material?" Then sit back and listen.

STAY ON TRACK

This is the flip side to the previous point. There's an art to facilitating an engaging conversation. While you want to leave space for group members to think through the discussion, you also need to keep your objectives in mind. Make sure the discussion is contributing to the bottom line for the week. Don't let the discussion veer off into tangents. Interject politely if you need to refocus the group. Also, if someone asks a question you don't know how to answer, it is generally best to admit it and move on.

MANAGE DISRUPTIONS

You may encounter challenges as you lead your group. Discussions can get off track. Group members may not be sensitive to the needs and ideas of others. Some might worry that they will be expected to talk about matters that make them feel awkward. Others may express comments that result in disagreements. So here are a few ground rules that can help ease this strain on you and the group.

First, if you find that one or two people are dominating the discussion time, direct a few questions to others in the group. Outside the main group time, ask the more dominating members to help you draw out the quieter ones. Work to make them part of the solution instead of part of the problem.

Second, when a disagreement occurs, encourage the group members to process the matter in love. Encourage those on opposite sides to restate what they heard the other side say, and then invite each side to evaluate if that perception is accurate. Lead the group in examining other passages related to the topic and look for common ground.

Above all, look to these words from Scripture: "Love one another" (John 13:34); "If it is possible, so far as it depends on you, live at peace with everyone" (Romans 12:18); "Whatever is true . . . noble . . . right . . . pure . . . lovely . . . admirable—if anything is excellent or praiseworthy—think about such things" (Philippians 4:8); and, "Everyone should be quick to listen, slow to speak and slow to become angry" (James 1:19). This will make your group time more rewarding and beneficial for everyone who attends.

PRAY

Finally, pray for your group time. This is the most important thing you can do as a leader. The best leaders get out of God's way and let him communicate through them. Remember: Books don't teach God's Word, and neither do sermons or discussion groups. God speaks into the hearts of people. Prayer is a vital part of communicating with him.

Pray for your group members. Pray for your own leadership. Pray that God is not only present at your group meetings but is directing them.

ABOUT CLAY SCROGGINS

Clay Scroggins is the bestselling author of *How to Lead When You're Not in Charge* and *The Aspiring Leader's Guide to the Future*. For over two decades he worked at North Point Ministries, starting as a facilities intern (aka Vice President of Nothing) and eventually becoming the lead pastor of their largest campus. Clay is now a sought-after leadership speaker, engaging audiences that include the Atlanta Hawks, Mercedes-Benz, Chick-fil-A, Federal Reserve Bank, and Terminus. Clay graduated from Georgia Tech with an industrial engineering degree and continued on to acquire a master's and doctorate from Dallas Theological Seminary. Clay and his wife, Jenny, have five children and live in Atlanta. For more information about Clay, visit clayscroggins.com.

How to Lead When You're Not in Charge

Leveraging Influence When You Lack Authority

Clay Scroggins

"This book will be one of the most, if not the most, pivotal leadership books you'll ever read." –Andy Stanley

"If you're ready to lead right where you are, this book can show you how to start." –Dave Ramsey

"Read this book! The marketplace is full of may helpful leadership messages, but this one is a standout." –Louie Giglio

One of the greatest myths of leadership is that you must be in charge in order to lead. Great leaders don't buy it. Great leaders lead with or without the authority and learn to unleash their influence wherever they are.

With practical wisdom and humor, Clay Scroggins will help you nurture your vision and cultivate influence, even when you lack authority in your organization. And he will free you to become the great leader you want to be so you can make a difference right where you are. Even when you're not in charge.

Available in stores and online!

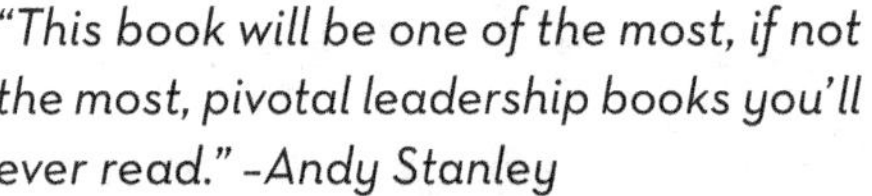
HarperChristian Resources

New Video Study for Your Church or Small Group

If you've enjoyed this book, now you can go deeper with the companion video Bible study!

In this six-session study, Clay Scroggins helps you apply the principles in *How to Lead in a World of Distraction* to your life. The study guide includes video notes, group discussion questions, and personal study and reflection materials for in-between sessions.

Study Guide
9780310115168

DVD
9780310115182

Available now at your favorite bookstore,
or streaming video on StudyGateway.com.

HarperChristian Resources